My Little Book of Rainbows and Daggers

I0104001

Agata Zema

chipmunkapublishing
the mental health publisher

Published by
Chipmunkapublishing
United Kingdom

http://www.chipmunkapublishing.com

ISBN   978-1-78382-173-0

Chipmunkapublishing gratefully acknowledge the support of Arts Council England.

Agata Zema is passionate about mental health and associated problems. She has shared one of her own stories in this book.

At the time of writing this book the author lived and worked in the Sunraysia Region in North West Victoria with her partner, son, and two dogs.

Agata is a counsellor, qualified in counselling & psychology and criminal psychology.

Agata Zema

Contents

Author's Note

This book is designed to be an 'easy' read, style-wise, without too much of the terminology and jargon used by professionals in this particular field. This is not a text book as such and should only be read as a basic starting point to familiarise the reader with various mental health problems as they are known today.

In addition, 'the real stories – the real people' overture is to provide an insight of how people with mental health problems are challenged on a daily basis to live a full and functioning lifestyle, without the extra difficulty presented by the prejudice and misunderstanding from those around them and the wider community.

This is a thought provoking and thought consuming read that will leave the reader feeling happily inflated at times and overwhelmed at other times. I cannot deny that some of the material from the stories will not shock or upset, but please read on, even if that means putting the book down for a few hours and regroup the thoughts and feelings generated. The reader may even ask why it had such an effect. The most likely reason may be due to fact that the experiences shared brought back memories and highlighted unresolved issues, pain and/or events and feelings long ago buried and not quite-so forgotten.

Overall, the experience should be viewed as positive enlightenment that should be felt and shared.

Objective

This book was written to give the reader some insight into mental health problems and how it affects people and their day to day activities.

Anybody can look up text book descriptions and definitions regarding mental health issues/illness/disorders, but that only gives the general public a very linear grasp of the reality associated with this topic.

Although one of the features of this book is a simplified version of what are some of the kinds of mental problems in the world today, the author's main objective was to compile real stories by real people. The author has included her own story, but felt it necessary to create an impact on the reader, by including other stories on a range of mental health problems. One story may appeal to the reader more than another, and in turn help channel a pathway to better equip them to seek and receive an appropriate level of help and support.

This book explores those who have or are still on their journey, living with mental health problems. The contributors express themselves through writing their stories, in their own unique way, in hope that they may reach others. 'You are not alone,' seems to be the common theme. In no way are their stories case studies, whereby information can be extracted, highlighted, rearranged and so on. The author was very careful to exercise the responsibility not to interfere with each story of experiences.
The result was to retain as much integrity and individualism as possible, making these genuine stories as believable as deserved.

The stories collected and compiled here, not only show courage and determination by the author, but just how harsh society can be. This overall lack of understanding or misunderstanding shared by a large percentage of the community, can produce fear, misjudgements, lack of support for those in need, segregation and stigmatism towards anyone going through a mental health issue or being diagnosed with a mental health problem. Hence the debate between 'survivors versus sufferers' issue arises. The individuals prefer to be known as 'survivors' whereas nearly everyone else refers to such as 'sufferers'. Whichever description is used by society, is not intended to be an insult, it is purely a subjective matter.

Majority of the stories featured here, were written for this book. With just a little encouragement and support, the majority of these stories were written down for the first time and many of the contributors felt a deep sense of relief and accomplishment, once completed. They also knew that they would be passing on their experiences to help others, the 'you are not alone,' theme was a major motivator.

It is guaranteed that at some stage, each one of us will come across mental health problems, whether it is directly or indirectly. Yourself, a family member, a boyfriend/girlfriend, relative, friend, work colleague, local acquaintance and/or even a celebrity may bring mental health 'to the table' for you.

A lot of society is not ready for a surprise insight into mental health problems, so the better informed, the better equipped to be either supported or supportive. In this way, a forewarned insight results in striving for early intervention which assists the affected individual to start living a happy and fulfilling life fuelled by achievable goals and dreams, earlier on in the journey, without the likelihood of losing what they have already loved and worked for.

Contributions –
Real Stories, Real People

Anonymous contributors were invited to share their experiences of mental health issues/illnesses/disorders, whether directly or indirectly, involved. For most of the contributions, the author is the diagnosed, and has put their life story into words in full, for the first time. I have encouraged them to keep to their own writing style, with little interference from me. Each story has its own impact and uniqueness not only because of this, but because the experiences are genuine. I have not selected case studies and nor have I selected information and data that I think is important. Each story will be appealing and intense in such a way to help cross the barriers between judgemental, unfounded views shared by many people who do not understand mental health problems and unite the community's courage to support and help those who need it the most.

Some authors have actually chosen to use their real, first names.

Some authors have gone that next step and supplied a favourite photo or image as part of their story, in an aid to reach out to the reader on more than one level.

Here is part sample of an invitation:

'...share your story, your journey from then to now. The objective of this book is to help others in the same or similar situation... it may assist them to seek the appropriate help, tell someone what they are going through and/or simply encourage them to want to get better, stay on medication, and commit to treatment plans....'

These invitations, in various forms, were posted online, in the local newspaper, community noticeboards and newspaper articles. Whichever form, the result proved worthwhile, attracting an interest from the public to write and share their story and/or look out for the book to digest an interesting read and gain a real insight into mental health.

hurt i go nowhere fast unpretty useless ignored misunderstood Alone unwanted alienated sad unloved ridiculed unheard Misguided misfit dismissed confused unlovable Misjudged tired Shapele...

'The Note'
By Maryanne

I got thin without realising it.

And then I got really skinny the same way. I was too busy taking in the new world around me. All strangeness and familiarity disguised as 'secondary college'. I was twelve years old and in my first year at a local Mildura school.

My home room teacher was fond of an activity that involved each student to draw a piece of paper out of a 'hat'. It was a get-to-know-you exercise in which one side of the piece of paper had a name of a student written on it and the other side was blank. We were expected to write something 'nice' on the blank side about the named student and immediately return the piece of paper back to the teacher.

For some reason girls found this task a lot easier to perform than the boys, no matter if the recipient was male or female. Also the boys would express their compliments in such a way that it was almost funny, like 'You seem ok' or 'You have a cool brother, he plays great football' and so on. The girls would write their message in curly writing with flowers for the dots in 'i' and draw smiley faces like☺. A compliment from a girl took on the form of 'I love your hair, how do you get it so shiny?' or 'you seem to be really good at sport'.

Every student pretended that this get-to-know-you activity was as boring as a maths class, but secretly we all enjoyed the anticipation and kept the pieces of paper as if they were miniature love letters.

One day that all changed for me.

'Anorexia' is read, in very neat hand writing. I later found out that that hand writing belonged to the teacher. It was a bit hard not to see the similarities of the writing on the whiteboard and that of the 'compliment' note.

I was so embarrassed, I had no idea what that meant. I made up something trivial at the time to pass onto my new friends in class. It was the 'done thing' to pass on the anonymous message to friends. Comply or forever be left behind. We all wanted to make and keep friends; after all, we were new students attending a new school.

Because of that one word, that one secret word, I already felt singled out and different. It carried a weight that was too heavy for me. I had to find out what that word meant. I did. At lunch time, I did the unthinkable and visited the library while my friends watched the boys kick the footy around the oval.

I read and reread the meaning and the small amount of literature that was known about the disorder at the time. I immediately thought that it is not me. I should not be ridiculed like this, my body, my business. I did not ask to be judged. Or be suddenly thrust into such confusion and frustration because someone could not mind their own business. Why not tell me face to face, at least we could have talked about it.

Anorexia Nervosa.

From that moment, everything around me changed, I changed. There was no question of turning back. I was forced to change, to see things differently and to see myself from an outsider's point of view. As a consequence, I developed a heightened awareness of how the teachers and students looked and talked to me. I was not paranoid or anything, obviously suspicious though. I just felt on my own and went into 'survival mode'.

Most of my memories of that time are clouded and laced with reflections and affected by other memory tampering. On the other hand, there are pockets of clarity, like it was only a short time ago, rather than the decades. On occasion, such memories invade my headspace uninvited, and I am then to stop and take note – again, to relive the experience.

These particular memories of such vividness have strong colour and smell associated with them. Along with how warm or cold it was that day, and whether the sun was shining brightly or if the sky and air was orange and gritty, tainted with dust from stirred up topsoil from surrounding fruit blocks and grain paddocks. Other times, I was confined to my room in the hospital.

During that first year at secondary college, I clearly remember sitting alone at recess and lunchtimes. Not really my doing. The parents of my friends and other students, told their children not to play or talk to me. They feared me and my condition a negative influence on their children. Are you for real? – I thought with amazement, it is not contagious. How sad. How sick and sad. Try being twelve and losing all your friends and unable to make new ones. It hurt. Still does.

Time passed like this. I juggled being alone, being avoided and unsure what to do about it. No way was I going to tell my parents, right?

On no particular awe inspiring day, a year 12 student started talking to me at lunchtimes. He was considered one of the coolest guys in the whole area, not just at school. At first he just stood next to me and said things like, 'Hi', 'How are you today?', 'What are my favourite subjects?' , ' Which teacher in Year 7 do I consider to be a real wet rag?' and so on. Looking back he was trying to communicate with me on the very first level, without jeopardising my comfort zone, trust and freedom of privacy if that is what I desired.

I was not at all concerned about this new situation. I was really grateful. I was relieved. I was happy that someone had the courage to reach out to me. So I was not invisible after all.

He did not fail me once. If he had other things to do, it did not matter, he always made time during the lunch breaks. Regardless of a five minute conversation or fifteen, we would talk or he would show me his artwork from class. He showed exceptional talent even at that age with only a few formal classes under his belt.

'Why do I 'eat' by myself?'
'Where are my friends?'
He asked one day.
I told him because I realised I needed help. I was not doing a very good job on my own. I told him about the 'compliment' note activity and what message was on my little piece of paper.

Wham!

His face showed such shock and anger that I thought I did the wrong thing by telling him about my Anorexia Nervosa and subsequent confusion. He could not believe I was alienated, with no follow-ups, no professional care which left me with no idea what to do.

'How can I help, what should I do for you, you can't go on like this, does your mum and dad know, has the teacher or principal talked to you yet...?'

Turning point.

The corridor of how I was no longer at school and admitted to the local public hospital for 'treatment' is still unclear to me, to this day. I was in hospital – why? I was not eating because I was not hungry because I was not happy. I was not obsessed with my body image in the mirror. I was not aware, at first, how my family reacted to all this. I did not have a clue why or what was going on. I am just me, no choice, just am.

There is that theory, which is a good one that emphasises that if you tell a young person, who commits unsociably acceptable activity, that he is a criminal, for example, and he gets thrown in prison, he will most likely become a 'better and more motivated' criminal. Like me, the more time I spent in the hospital, the more I learnt what was expected of me, as a sufferer of Anorexia Nervosa. I learnt how to think and behave as one. I was continuously punished for 'acting' as expected by the staff. But, that is all they knew at the time. This disorder was in its infancy, at the time, in regards to diagnosis and treatment. Apparently, I was the youngest sufferer that they have had to deal with and the staff always had to consult with specialised staff from the big cities. Except for my paediatrician, two nurses and one hospital janitor, the rest of the staff viewed me as a 'time waster'.

'Just eat and put on weight, what's so hard about that?'

'Help' at that time, with the limited and primitive resources and workable treatment plans that were on offer were administered in 'good faith.' Isolation was one technique. If I did not gain a certain amount of kilograms per day, I was banned from seeing my family, relatives, games, books, the playroom with the wall to wall blackboard, other patients, any gifts that were for me were simply left at the nurse's station and the nurses encouraged not to linger for a chat when they entered my room.

I filled in my time, when exposed for days on end under this treatment regime, by counting the holes in the hospital ceiling. Over and over I repeated the counting, my eyes hurt with the effort.

The other form of 'treatment' was the high calorie food for every meal. For me, this was even worse than the isolation technique. Seriously, did the staff really think this would encourage me to come to my senses and eat and put on weight and be cured? This was forced on me constantly. The quicker I put on weight, the quicker I would leave the hospital, the quicker my disorder would no longer exist. That was the initial theory.

I craved for fresh fruit and vegetables. I come from a European background, which utilises fresh produce of the season, prepared simply. How I loved to eat a plate of steamed bitter greens. Every request I made, I was turned down. Instead, I was given things like sugar with cornflakes, milkshakes that were two thirds sugar, greasy potato, battered fish, crumbed protein of some sort and an indescribable custard-looking dessert. The milkshake I used to pour straight down the sink, mostly sugar, then syrup and some milk. I had to rinse the cup out a few times with water just to get the sugary sludge out. Even the biggest sugar addict would not go near that drink.

Naturally, I stopped eating altogether. The food was awful. My refusal to put any hospital food in my mouth really worked on the staff's resources of what to do next. The stomach tube was their answer. This tube was shoved as carefully as possible, up my nose and down the oesophagus into my stomach. If I coughed that indicated that the tube was entering the airway passage instead and the whole process started over. The fluid that was then pumped into me was freezing, I could feel the flow the whole time until my stomach warmed it up. That fluid was brown and thick. Brown and stinky when it gave me diarrhoea, this was quite often.
One part of this force feeding technique did get me to put on weight, quickly. Then I would be sent home. The staff's main objective for treatment was weight gain only. How things have changed for treatment now! Because I was sent home straight away, within days I would lose the weight again. How was I meant to maintain and keep gaining weight after a steady diet of high calorie food – when I ate it and the force feed of brown fluid via the stomach tube?

After this ritual of admission and discharge, the staff finally woke up to a pattern. Go figure!
From that time of awakening, I was allowed to see visitors more often, receive their gifts instead of them being left at the nurse's station and forgotten about, and was able to freely walk around the ward.

I got used to being supervised constantly. My solution was for me to retreat into my own world. I had to find a place, while I was in hospital, to feel comfortable and have thoughts that did not revolve around food, weight, how much I missed my family, how much I wanted to go back to school and the fear of punishment.

With this new outlook on treatment, I was glad and saddened when my family came to visit me more often. I wanted to go home too. My school principal came when she could and gave me a beautiful necklace to remind me that I am in people's thoughts and prayers. She wanted to help more, but did not know how. From then until many years later, she always took a keen interest in my health and wellbeing. The students from my class also came to see me once or twice, bearing gifts to fill in my day, like word find books. The outside world was finally reaching me. Up until then I had felt like I was going to be isolated forever.

One day, soon after being 'touched' by the outside world, things changed.

I was sick of being in hospital.
I was sick of the awful food.
I was sick with hurt about not seeing my family every day. Homesick.
I was sick of the fear of being punished.
I was sick of the sight of scales.
I was sick of being talked about but not 'to.'
I was sick of not being with people, and with people my own age. I wanted to run around and laugh and play and learn new things at school.
I was sick of having no friends.

Out of the blue, I got a special treat. I was allowed home for the weekend, after quite a long hospital stay. This was my chance to escape this unnatural atmosphere of recovery and 'rehabilitation.'
As soon as I got home, I opened the fridge door and just stood there looking at all the food.
I was not disgusted or anything, at the sight of all that food. I just picked up a plate of pasta with a variety of vegetables stirred through, that was left over from the night before, and ate it with my fingers.

I ate. I did not lick, nibble, spit it back out or throw the food in the bin. I ate.

I never went back to the hospital. My family took over my first line of support along with the paediatrician and the psychologist I had been seeing during my treatment in hospital. My paediatrician was a saint that always smiled and had all the time in the world for me. He treated me and my family with respect and compassion. He too was trying very hard to find better ways to go about treatment. Not just the weight gain aspect, but nutrition, better thought patterns and other ways to suit me, as a young individual.

My psychologist was not so outwardly confident. I could tell he was trying to think instead of talk whenever we had a session. To make these experiences less uncomfortable for me, I would tell him what he wanted to hear. He really did try to be creative in his approaches, but he was still tied down to his standardised treatment procedures and expected text book outcomes. Overall, he was harmless but not really that helpful.

I was now recovering. I felt stronger and my general wellbeing was improving. I could go back to school. My 'friends' were my friends again and their parents did not feel threatened by me anymore.

Although it was a difficult and long journey, I was one of the lucky ones. For many reasons because some Anorexia Nervosa sufferers die, some get cancer of the stomach or tongue, then die and others have to nurse the consequences of having the disorder, either mental issues or physical ones like, weak hearts, stomach problems and so on.

To this day I remain fit and healthy. No relapses. I have accepted what happened to me and moved on. No denial to impede rehabilitation and recovery. I accept me, understanding me is another story.

By Maryanne

'Bitter
Sweet'
By
Sheryl

Introduction

Depression, Anxiety, Alcoholism and Suicide, Post Natal Depression, all of these illnesses have been or are still part of my life. The effect of them on me has and still is massive.

When I was diagnosed with anxiety in 2010. I was very fortunate to find a doctor who was understanding, and cared for me so wonderfully I thank her for saving me and getting me back on track.

I take a small dose of an anxiety drug today and feel great.
When first diagnosed I had two visits with a psychologist and I found him very helpful.

To try to help me to understand my anxiety, I began to write down my story from my very first childhood memory and it soon become apparent where my problems began.

I was born in 1952.I am my father's second child and my mother's fourth child.

My father is my mother's second husband, sadly she lost her first husband in the 2nd world war he was a POW in a Japanese prison camp on Ambon Island, they had two children together; my beautiful sister and a brother who I never met , he passed away in 1949 aged 12years not long after my parents married.
My mother came from a family of 10, was born and raised in the Mallee, she described a wonderful childhood with lots of fun and parties and bits of mischief.

My father the middle of his three siblings lived and was raised on a fruit block. His father was a very strict man and his mother immaculate, they expected the very best from their children in every way.

Sadly my father and his older sister and younger brother all died from suicide before my Grandmother passed away in 1980. Their father had died in 1956.

What has become very clear to me is we are all victims of our circumstances.

However it is where we take ourselves from there that makes the difference.

I have had the ability to analyse my life from a very young age, so from a very young age I decided what I wanted from life.

When my husband and I met it didn't take us long to realise we shared very similar backgrounds, when we became engaged to be married we made a vow to each other;

that we would never bring our children up to suffer the neglect and drunken violence we had been subjected to.

We have three beautiful children and tried to expose them to the good and bad things in life from the safety of our fold. We gave them love and freedom as young teenagers and adults and they have grown into responsible and loving parents, we share a great amount of our time together with them and our five grandchildren.

We have some lively discussions at times and everyone is not always on best terms.

 But in times of crises we can forget our differences and come together as one family.

 I am proud of them I am proud of my Husband and I am proud of myself.
This is the family life I craved for as a child. I love that I have been able to give it to them.

Being the daughter of an alcoholic it is no surprise to me that my journey to find my ancestors would begin with my Great Great Great Grand Father being a publican and landlord of the White Hotel in Plank Road also listed as Main Road Ballarat circa 1863 the road is between Ballarat and Buninyong. This   area was the focus of the start of the Gold Rush and many Hotels etc. sprang up there. I am not surprised to find it would be my g.g.g.grandfather that would be enterprising enough to know that there would be money to be made selling alcohol, rather than food.

LIVING IN SOUTH MERBEIN 1954-1956

My earliest child hood memory of my father was hiding behind a huge lounge chair in the dark because he was on a violent rampage with a loaded shot gun, he had fired shots into a tin plate he had hung on the wire fence that surrounded our home. With the sound of those shots still ringing in my head, my sisters and my mother hid behind the chair in the dark, I can't clearly remember the reason for his outrage but it had something to do with his meal that night, I was scared so scared not for me! But for my mother who I knew was his target. And all I could think of was I needed to protect her, this was the pattern that followed for the rest of my life. My father finally left mum and moved in with his mother in the early 1970's. The instinct to protect my mother stayed with me until she died at the age of 97 in 2010

Despite living in fear from such a young age, I have some fond memories of life in South Merbein. We lived in a small cottage on the fruit block owned by my Grand Parents, my Grand Mother was a wonderful gardener and even better cook. Picking time was a busy time with tractors, and dip tins and the huge hot dip that the fruit was dipped in before it was put on the drying racks, the pickers were mostly from Italy or Greece. I was forbidden to go out of our house gate, but I knew if I waited all day at that gate I would get my reward. Twice a day at 10 am in the morning, and 3pm in the afternoon on the dot, my nana would come past with the pickers smoko, I would be so excited and busting inside, as she came to my gate I would pester her to go to smoko with her but the answer was always it's no place for a little girl you wait by the gate if there is any smoko left you can have it on my way back, without fail on her return there would always be a cake left over for me. I like to think she had packed one especially for me any way, my favorite was jelly cake I can still see that little red jelly cake, she would hand it through the wire gate to me, and that little cake made me so happy all my fears disappear for the rest of the day.
I do not know if she knew how badly her son treated my mother, but surely, my grandparents must have heard all the fighting and yelling, surely they would not have ignored the screams of fear coming from their small grandchildren. Is that why my mother hated her in-laws so much? Is that why my mother taught us to hate them? And instilled in us that we were scum teaching us our surname name was poison. I don't know. What I do know is that I loved my Nana despite the fact that to love Nana was to betray my mother who I had to protect from my father the man who I had grown to hate. And all this before the age of 4years old.

My Grandfather Alf died when I was four years old. I have only two memories of him. I can remember him sitting in the garden on a wooden garden seat. My eldest sister was with me we were going to town, which was a 20 k trip and always took forever he gave us some coins to spend. The other memory of him is still me today we were in the kitchen. Nana was washing the dishes Grandfather and

I had a tea towel each and he was singing to me. Wash the dishes dry the dishes turn the dishes over,
I often wonder if these memories stayed with me because my mother always portrayed him as a mean man.

She hated everything about him and my Grandmother, my Grandfather was the boss and everyone feared him, my nana was a hard worker and immaculate in everything she did cooking, gardening, sewing you name she could do it.
Any way it doesn't matter to me now I still have my two nice memories of him.

LIVING IN DARETON FROM 1956

After my Grandfather died in 1956 the property at South Merbein was sold and my Grandmother moved into a house in Eleventh Street in Mildura. My parents brought a house in Dareton. Dad had a job at the Mildura Co- Op where they packed Dried Fruit and Citrus.

Our lives took a downhill slide from the day we moved to Dareton, my father had begun to drink heavily on a daily bases to the point that in the late 1960 he lost his job.

My father was coming home drunk most nights; he would go straight to the pub or club after work at 5.00 o'clock and come home at teatime I think it was 7.00 o'clock closing in those days. As I heard him drive into our shed, my stomach would start to knot up because I knew there would be an argument that always lead to him hitting mum. My sisters and I would get in between them to stop the fight, he never hit us kids but mum needed to go to the doctor for bruising on many occasions. It wasn't happening just at night but all weekends too. If he was home I couldn't go and play in the street with the other kids because I feared for my mother's safety, I hoped the neighbours didn't hear the arguments, but I am sure they knew what was going on.

On so many nights mum or my sister would call the police, the town had a Sergeant and a Constable in those days both knew my father so it was even more embarrassing for us when we needed their help. Most of the time they would take him and lock him up for the night sometimes it lead to him going to AA meetings but that never lasted long he would still go straight to the club and have a lemonade , all I wanted was for him to come home and spend time with us like other families. I just don't understand how he had no fatherly or protective instinct toward us. He blamed us girls for the lawns not being mowed and complained that our garden wasn't neat like others in the town. I took the guilt on board for many years until I was old enough to realise. It was not my fault I was a little girl how was I meant to keep up with the gardens and house maintenance. Sometimes the fights were so bad Mum would sleep in my bed we would all get in together safety in numbers, he would come in ranting when he could see he wasn't able to get a punch in on Mum he would call us all bitches in our bitches nest.

It wasn't long before Mum started to join him at the club I think it was about the same time as they started to play bowls they were both good bowlers Mum was especially good and won many prizes my father hated that she was better than he was.

All their weekends were spent in the club and most weekdays. We would be left at home by ourselves at night we were so scared. My youngest sister was only about 4 and my eldest sister was left in charge of her and me. I would have been about 6 and my eldest sister about 8. My youngest sister and I would beg mum to stay home, and she would call us selfish for not letting her have some time to herself, that would have been fine if it wasn't most nights and there would be peace when they got home, but no every night same old fight. I would lay awake in my bed ready to fly out to the kitchen to get between them and break it up. I don't know how many times the phone got ripped out of the wall and his dinner plate was thrown at him as he staggered into the kitchen, or how often he hit the neighbours tin fence trying to park the car in the shed, he was so bad an alcoholic he had sherry bottles hidden in the back yard and in the shed. He would go outside at all hours of the night for a sly nip this meant that he was drunk all of the time, he refused to bath, shave or change his clothes, he always smelt of cigarette smoke and alcohol. Both those smells churn my stomach to this day.

I began school at the beginning of term when I turned 5. My Mother arranged for the next door neighbour to take me and her daughter on my first day, I don't remember much of my first year at school but I grew to hate it, I was frightened, shy, timid confused and could not concentrate. I spent all my school days hiding the shame that I felt for my family life, my father was a drunk my mother went to the club and our house was a dump, I never invited friends to my house to play as I was so ashamed of the way we lived so I withdrew inside myself. I now realise the reason for my learning difficulties was the stress of the night before and the fear that while I was at school my father would harm my mother and it would be my fault because I hadn't been there to protect her.

My father's alcoholism became so bad that he lost his job, then left my mother. I don't remember whether he willingly left or she asked him to go. He went to live with his mother, but would show up at home unexpectedly now and again.

I was married by now and my husband and I had bought a small cottage that backed onto my family home with a lane way in between. The last time he turned up unannounced my sister and her 4 children were visiting my mother. My father was drunk and aggressive so mum and my sister when to visit a friend hoping he would leave. Meanwhile my husband was working down near our back fence. I was inside our house when my husband came running in to me yelling your father is in the shed he has a shot gun to his head. In shock and with my heart beating so loud in my head I ran to the shed just as he pulled the trigger and slumped back in the chair he was sitting in. The doctors told us he survived that time because of the angle of the gun. He had extensive facial wounds that required a lot of surgery while he was in hospital he was able to receive counselling and rehabilitation. But I am afraid he could never beat the alcohol, and spent his last years as a derelict drinking with a collection of homeless men and derelicts in the parks and gardens around town. It was pitiful to see him like that, my heart ached for his mother. It was about 3 years after he had tried to commit suicide that I received a message through my neighbour from my grandmother that my father had passed away, the autopsy report said he died as a result of an overdose of his prescribed medication. At his funeral I cried and cried I thought I would never stop. Some of my tears were for his and my sad miserable lives, and some were relief now one of the reasons for my misery was gone. I now know the meaning of **"Bitter Sweet"**.

To be continued.

By Sheryl

'*MY*
STORY,
EX-USER/ABUSER
TURNS
LIFE AROUND
FOR THE BETTER'
BY
C.SMITH

I am a 26 year old female living in a small country town of Mildura, Victoria! Three years ago in 2007 I was a heavy drinker and a heavy user (marijuana) I would work 6am till 2pm and the minute I finished I would race home to smoke copious amounts of weed and wine till I passed out, this had been going on for years! Nothing had happened I wasn't hurting anyone so I continued! Me and my partner (a former smoker) had been planning to backpack overseas to live in England! We saved for a year and the time to jester was approaching very fast and I was smoking more than ever! The night before we were to travel to Melbourne to catch our 24 hour long flight to London I had smoked three billies and laid down, somewhat my thoughts were racing about the plane crashing and suicide bombers being on my plane, I went outside to calm down and have a smoke but this overwhelming feeling was taking over my body I was shaking I could feel my heart pounding and I was sweating I honestly thought I was dying so I drove myself to outpatients at the hospital by this time I was really freaking out! After a long wait for any one a doctor called me in I reckon I had paced up and down 1000 times, he asked me what was wrong and I said I am dying! They hooked me up to all these machines and told me there was nothing wrong at that I was having a panic attack gave me one Valium and sent me home! I struggled with this so called anxiety for five years trying to work out natural remedies and non-pill diets but all failed not until I fell pregnant to my new partner that I was that scared of the pregnancy. A little nurse gave me a little white pill 100mg of Sertrelene and it all went away 12 months later and I have not had one panic attack! And a beautiful 12 month old princess! Seek help it worked for me.

C.Smith

'Post natal
depression, my
journey'
By Amber

My partner and I were 16 and 17 years old when we discovered that we were expecting our 1st baby. Skylar Anne-marie* was born on July 4th 2010 at 3:26am, almost exactly 8 pounds! I had been dating my boyfriend for 2 and half years by the time she arrived. Despite an emotionally difficult pregnancy, she was the best thing that had ever happened to me and I absolutely adore her to this day.

It was about 6 months after Skylar's birth that I really began to feel overwhelmed, I was sad all the time, and when I wasn't sad I just felt numb, lost in my own endless thought's that made no sense... It was the worst feeling of helplessness. All I could think was 'what's happening with me, I have a beautiful baby daughter, supportive partner and loving family, what the hell is wrong with me???' My mood swings, tiredness and lack of interest in anything began to destroy my relationships from the inside out. I was alone (not literally, but that's how I felt) PND robbed me of my ability to enjoy anything; it stole away friends, fun and made me feel totally isolated. I don't remember how old my baby daughter was when I was finally diagnosed. But I think she was around 8 or 9 months old...

I grew up with a Mother who suffered from Bi-Polar Disorder, and as a child I vowed to never let a mental illness take over my life... But of course PND doesn't care about your plans; you can be the kindest, happiest person in the world... and still get sick. It also does not make you a bad Mum!

Me and my boyfriend had been together for over 3 years and had just got engaged when we broke up, he couldn't handle it anymore... he said to me that I wasn't the same person he fell in love with. I wasn't myself. He moved out and this totally broke my heart, I didn't know what to do. I looked at my baby girl one morning and just cried.

I made an appointment with my local GP and she diagnosed me with Post Natal Depression. I felt relieved as she referred me to a mental health professional and I was prescribed 50mg of sertraline per day. I went to visit my ex, who I was still helplessly in love with and needed him more than anything at this time in my life. I cried and cried as I told him I had PND, it was hard for me to accept, I hated not being in control of my own body! But the worst wasn't over yet!

Anti-depressant medication often makes your symptoms worse before they get better. I had been on my medication for only a week when I started having thoughts of self-harm and crazy ideas to leave the state and just run away. I packed some stuff for me and my baby and went to visit my ex again, so that he could spend some time with our daughter. I could see that being away from me and his baby was hard for him, but he made it clear that he couldn't handle things at home. I don't think either of us believed it would ever get better.

That day, I called my mum asking her to please take care of my daughter, because I didn't trust myself with her. I phoned the hospital and they did their best to reassure me that I was fine... but I wasn't! I couldn't stop thinking all these horrible things I wanted to do to myself. I wanted to die, and I meant it! I took a handful of my anti-depressants (maybe 3 or 4 four more than I'm supposed to). I knew I hadn't taken enough to do any harm but somehow at least in the moment, I felt in control! My mum came to pick my daughter up, but I decided to go with her and spend the night with family. I lay in my little sister's bed for hours, checking my phone hoping or a message from my ex, and staring at the ceiling. The lonely, pathetic, worthless feeling was back again. Two mental health workers came to my mums home to speak to me; they were caring and seemed genuinely concerned for my wellbeing. They upped my dose of medication to 100mg and only gave me 3 pills at a time so that I couldn't seriously overdose myself. I had appointments twice a week for a month so they could keep an eye on me. It helped, and for the 1st time in a year I didn't feel totally hopeless.

As the turmoil that was my emotions slowly got better, my Ex-boyfriend and I began to reconcile our relationship, although he still did not want to move home. I was on an emotional roller-coaster! I still had days of feeling like shit and crying for no good reason, but there were good days too. My ex-boyfriend moved home later that month and things improved. It was a long month even with him home. All up it was 3 months from the time I was diagnosed before I felt my (pre-pregnancy) self again, my boyfriend was happy, my baby was happy and healthy and finally, I was too.

When I reflect of those times I thank god it's over, I would never wish that kind of hardship on anyone! My boyfriend had only moved out for 3 weeks, but part of me will always be mad at him for leaving me at such an awful time. But I know he made the right decision, if he hadn't left I may never have made the decision to get help. Everything just started to fall into place and we decided that we were ready to plan our wedding (again).

November 16th 2011, four years to the day that we began dating, my boyfriend and I got married! It's so weird to think that we started that year so awfully and yet ended it so happily. Our Daughter is now 32 months old (two and a half) and as beautiful as ever! My Husband and I have been married for over a year now and recently celebrated the arrival of our second child, a lovely baby boy Cayden James, born October 29th 2012. I am now 20 and still on my anti-depressants. My doctor says now is a good time to reduce my dosage and eventually come off medication altogether. I take care to do things that I enjoy and focus on keeping myself mentally well. I limit my alcohol intake to maybe 3 drinks on a weekend, as alcohol and depression isn't a good mix! I enjoy weekends with friends, visiting family and working as a photographer. My Husband and two wonderful children are all the motivation I need! I hope this story gives other mums out there hope that with the right doctors, support and medication, things will get better!

By Amber

'Fire with Fire, my life story' By India

For such a long time I have felt that I should be able to tell my life story publicly so I can lift a weight off my shoulders and so people stop judging without knowing me and I think it's a strong choice and I am proud so here I go.

I remember when I was little, not even 3, my uncle terry would see me every day and treat me like his own daughter. He would bring me presents and cuddle and kiss me and he gave me a wombat I still have to this day. He wore black shirts with wolves on them and he was like a second dad to me. I remember one day mum and dad told me he died and went to a special place and I packed a suit case and cried in a corner praying and begging to be with him because I felt like it was my fault he killed himself. My dad was broken. Mum would see his ghost and everyone knew about his suicide. At such a young age I understood it all and every day since I'd have nightmares. Every time I got in trouble and was sent to my room as a child around 5 I'd see his ghost in the mirror and he would promise me they loved me and that it wasn't my fault. That suicide ruined me and my family. As I grew older I became more fond of ghosts and spiritual things. I would make spells and wish for things and I would turn to fairies in my yard. In primary school and kinder I got teased for it all. I'd spend my playtimes talking to birds and collecting pine cones. I'd believe my uncle was there. Besides all this, primary school was my change. I became so obsessed with being cool and fitting in. At 10 I had puppy fat and round glasses and every day I would get told I was fat. I wouldn't eat my packed lunch and I'd throw it in the bin so mum thought I ate it. I brang make up to school to look pretty and I'd get out of class to spew when more kids told me I was fat. That's when my anorexia and bulimia started. No one knew about it at all. But it was better that way. Throughout all of primary school to grade six I was told I was fat and ugly and that no boy would wanna kiss me ever. I had no self-confidence. In grade six, my nan died from golden staph and no one really cared at all. After the funeral I sat at with no emotion I went to school and I locked myself in the toilet and spewed and cried for a few hours and no one really knew. I had to pretend I wasn't crying but then the principal found me and I went home. Death really rocked me. But as I hit year 7 I cut myself for the first time and still starved because every girl was pretty and when I found love in parkway drive I got spat at and rocks thrown at me. But I remember I thought I felt happiness within a group of girls. We were friends and used to talk on piczo and msn. After a while I started to get abuse on piczo for being fat and ugly and on msn my 'friends' sent me convos from other girls saying I should kill myself because I was flat chested and ugly. I really did nothing and really thought I found safety within people in high school. It all got taken to the police and school and these girls never spoke to me again. I started to find boyfriends and my first one used me and cheated on me and broke up with me because I was afraid to do sexual things. But at this point I was 14 and still hadn't done anything sexual which was a good thing back then. I really began to find myself at this age and after being a blonde I dyed my hair black and changed who I was. People saw my legs and arms and at lunch times I'd have random boys pull my sleeves up and ask if I was emo and they would search for new cuts. I would walk to school to lose weight and I wouldn't spend my lunch cash because I wanted it for cigarettes because I was getting into it because it took away stress and helped me lose weight. A few years later at 15 turning 16 soon, I found a boy who I thought loved me. I fought for him and was in a rocky situation with my family. He would listen and tell me I looked shit and then would be lovely and to be honest I really thought that's what love was. Throughout this whole five months relationship I was getting molested at school by a boy a few years older than me. Every day he would follow me and touch my boobs and try and go up my skirt. I tried to tell the boy I was with but the guy who molested me was always at his house and I knew he wouldn't believe me. After the guy stalked for my number and threw me up on a locker and touched my vagina I had the guts to finally tell someone which was Gavin Dunbar. I cried and the police were called. I really thought I was alone in this and I made a statement and broke my parent's hearts. I wagged school and for months I waited for the police to give me court details. Throughout this my boyfriend left me and told me to kill myself. He then told everyone I lied about being molested and the guy who molested me, his sister tried getting people to bash my family. As if it wasn't hard enough I belted her. Still to this day I have trouble with the family and being touched sexually. I still live in fear. A year after all the bullshit I went to Tafe and saw this guy who touched me get hit by a girl and I found out 24 cases were against him and I wasn't alone because a lot of my friends were in the same situation. I kept to myself for a while and in year 11 at senior I felt so alone with new people around me and no one to listen. In February, a guy named Lachlan Bailey decided to be friend me because he saw me as the most perfect person. He thought I was a model. For a few months we liked each other and we went through the same shit. At this point of time I was weighing 43kg and was smoking drugs, slashing and burning myself and Lach was the same which was such a closure for me. He would speak to me every day and would tell me he loved me. We both had the same issues and he told me everything about his life and as did I. After a bit he was in hospital due to being mentally ill and came back and was my valentine. In march we spent his last day together and he showed me his tablets and told me he'd leave and I said I would leave too but I needed him here and I told him I understood his problems and we smoked and sung together. The next day I woke up to being invited to rip pages and I found out he did it. He did it. He was dead. And I was ruined. I went to school in tears and fell into my girlfriends arms at the time and cried. I was so mentally unstable that I shared our last day to people. That week I had girls pull me out of class and tell me it was my fault. I had 33 people tell me in a day that it should have been me cause I let him die. That night I got stoned and greened out. I went to school a few days after and some girls gave me a note from Lach saying thanks and he was sorry.

No one spoke to me besides one boy who was very popular. He let me know it would be okay and I was beautiful. A week later it was Lach's funeral and I had to go with several counsellors and my parents so I didn't get beaten up. The whole funeral I cried and I really felt alone again. I felt as though my life wasn't worth it. The boy who cared for me held my hand and took me to him to cry. We became closer and in such an unstable time he got into my mind and heart and found out everything about me, took my virginity that was so sacred to me and left me. I tried to kill myself after. I took numerous sheets of pills and weighed 36kg and slashed myself in the shower until I got dizzy. I then forced myself to spew and tried to detox myself because I was afraid of hurting my family like my uncle did. I told the guy I liked and he didn't care. As I was hated through school senior in year 11 one person actually took the time to know me and ignored his family and friends hatred for me and actually cared like Lach did. When I cried at school he'd hold me and when I wagged to do drugs he'd be there with me and when I felt alone he would tell me I was beautiful and that he actually loved me. I felt like it was a lie and I tried to kill myself again. And I let him know because I thought I was pregnant because after losing my virginity I hadn't got my period for ages. I was scared and wanted to die. This boy Xavier cried and was so afraid and talked me out of it and detoxing again. Xav and I became closer and I shared a lot with him and not once did he judge me. He always cared. One day we sat together and he realised I weighed less and that my bones in my legs and face were visible and my thigh gap was 20cm and he talked me into eating. Slow eating. I would eat a chip or a chicken strip. But that was a start. Even though he helped me he started to smoke and do drugs too and I felt bad. One day on May 19th he asked me, to be his girlfriend and I said yes and today in 13 days will be Xavier's and my 21 months.

Besides all the shit I went through, despite the fact I don't self-harm and I now weigh 55kg, art helped me cure the addictions I had. Whenever I felt and feel down I draw. I paint. I sketch. And to this day, people are buying my art and asking me to design them tattoos. In 2 weeks I start my art diploma.

A lot of kids tell me I am an inspiration. But the truth is that even though I seem happy always. I still want to be thinner at times and I still want to hurt myself at times. But that's life. You grow from your experiences and if it wasn't for Gavin Dunbar, Lachlan Bailey, Xavier I 'Anson and my family, I really would not be here today.

So before judging me because of my weight or art or opinions, here's my story. Make sure you know it before judgement.

Thanks.

By India

'A true story about me feeling alone and sad' By Margaret

My husband and I have become no more than roommates. While he seems perfectly content this has made me incredibly unhappy and sad to the point I am considering leaving. I don't want to live like this any longer. For many years we couldn't keep our hands off on another, always taking any opportunity to have sex but now....we do nothing, been 6 years, no sex. We talk about nothing of meaning, we don't cuddle or hold hands and it's been literally years since he has taken me out for dinner. He has grown distant and uninterested in improving our marriage. Last year I kept asking him to go away for a long weekend to work on our marriage. I read a couple of marriage books. He knew this but never once asked about them. Not once has he ever asked about what I learned or how we can make our marriage better and get back on track. As for going away for a weekend, the timing was never right, according to him. He couldn't take off work. For a while I thought he was having an affair but I now know that isn't the case. He insists that it's not me and he will not go to a doctor to see if there is a medical issue with him. He just seems to be content with the situation.

I told my parents that I am so unhappy and I want to break up but they always try to make it work but it can't work no more.

At this point I have now checked out this marriage. The current situation is not the way I want to live. I am still young and I want passion in my life. I want to feel wanted and desired. I want to sit across a candle light table and be told that I'm beautiful. I want romance.

By Margaret

'The Scales of Imbalance' By Mari

I can't remember when they started, but the headaches were constant 24/7 which interfered with my sleep. I had strange dreams that stayed with me, of large rolling balls, babbling voices, large shapes moving, maybe the headaches were connected.

I left home at 17 after an altercation with my father and moved into a house with 3 others, organised by social services.

After meeting my future husband, 12 months later I was seeing a chiropractor, at times, daily, for some relief for the headaches.

I don't really recall when the headaches stopped, but it wasn't thanks to the chiro.

When I was about 43 I had strange flickers of dizziness, I was also having panic attacks and started to miss appointments and cancelling at the last minute, and avoiding functions.

After a lot of scans and tests I was finally diagnosed with depression and put on antidepressants which immediately stopped the dizzying.
When I was about 46, I experienced the death of my parent's marriage after 35 yrs. The next 18 months were hell with me as the eldest acting as go between. Mum tried to commit suicide and then not long after my son in law was killed in an attack and I had to cope with my daughter's venting, she became bitter, hard and selfish, like it was all about her and I couldn't do enough for her. It was all too much so we moved house, 4 hrs drive away.

Now my sister and brother are going through hell with mum's tantrums, dad's heart surgery and prolonged illness, their financial woes....and now I can worry and feel guilty from afar.

I feel useless; I seem to focus on what I can't do. I find it difficult to focus on what I can. Although deep down I know I would feel better if I look on the 'bright side' of things.

I am a chronic pain sufferer, particularly the last few months the pain has become almost unbearable. I have suffered back pain with spasms for years, but the pain is worse now. It distracts me no end. The pain and stiffness prevents me from enjoying life and what is around me.

I am on medication for depression. I used to self-medicate, not anymore of course. I used to juggle 5 tablets, now with the GP's advice; I only have 2 in the mornings. If I miss my dose or try to get off them, I get flooded with emotions. I must do. I do not really 'feel' it. I would have tears running down my face and not even realise I am crying for example.

I have started and stopped pain killers of all types by they don't work or the side effects are too awful for me to put up with. So I stop taking them. But the pain I physically feel is extremely unpleasant and consumes me, mind and body.

I take medication for other things as well. So I juggle a lot of unwontedness daily, although it seems I do not have a choice. Where is my relief?

My relief is that my wonderful husband of 37 years is my best friend and my unfailing support. He is definitely my rock and has been with me every single step or leap of the way. How fortunate am I to have him by my side unconditionally. He knows me, everything, even the gambling I don't like admitting to.

I have a very strong need to nurture and am constantly bringing home some animal, I also do foster care, it's such a wonderful experience to be there and be needed by these 'little dependents.' I am smiling now just thinking about it. It makes me feel good and wanted and capable and happy.

But I tend to be very impulsive and not think ahead about the consequences.

At the moment my constant is pain.   I have just enough determination to heal, if my pain will subside somehow.

The few 'normal' days I have now and then, are worth striving for. The sun does indeed come up every morning.

My future is a 'Work in Progress'.

By Mari

'Not giving up on myself – in black and white'

Hey.

My name is Candice Adams. This is my story and how I managed to change my life despite my mental health disorders.

My whole life I was physically abused by my mum. I was put into foster care at the age of ten and that's when my 'symptoms' began to show. I was never able to concentrate or cope with barely anything. If a teacher changed I would break down or I would act out aggressively or violently. I was never able to sit still or process things properly and couldn't handle being ruled by people that meant nothing to me.

At the age of thirteen I found that nicotine helped me control myself and helped me relax a little but as I got older, my symptoms just got worse and worse.

By fifteen I wasn't in school, I was being arrested all the time, throwing myself at boys and men and was relying on alcohol and cannabis to control my emotions and actions.

I was forced into counselling as I was regularly attempting suicide and self harming.

At sixteen I finally got diagnosed with depression but with the way I was feeling and the way I was going about things I knew it was more than that.

I fell pregnant at sixteen and didn't want my baby to be like me so I accepted the help that was being provided. I attended regular counselling. I trialed several medications and got help when I felt like I needed it. I gave up the drugs and alcohol and was doing what I had to. Then I gave birth to her. Children Protection stepped in and took my baby. I hit the drugs again and started self harming and thinking about suicide. I admit I was trying to get her home but not as much as I should have been. After nearly a year of my daughter being in foster care I fell pregnant again. This time I stopped all my drinking and drug taking and self harming for good. I wanted to provide the best I could for this baby and not have a reason for CP to step in. Unfortunately my baby didn't make it full term but my heart was set to not get back to the way I was. Fifteen and a half months later. I am still off the drugs. I very rarely drink and I no longer dependent on my medication. I am finally happy with my life. I was told several times that the alcohol and drugs were dragging me down but I kept denying it. As soon as I gave it all up, for my girls I felt better. I still have them days where I feel like utter trash but I get through them. I think that what made me the way I was back then, was my childhood, I always felt down in the dumps feeling sorry for myself. My kids have taught me that I have to keep moving forward and the more I focus on my future the better I feel. I have now been diagnosed with Borderline Personality Disorder, Post Traumatic Stress Disorder, Depression, Severe Anxiety and Substance Abuse Disorder. But I can and HAVE dealt with my coping strategies and have learned to deal with it. GOOD LUCK EVERYONE, WE CAN GET THROUGH IT!!

Impressions

It was a welcome challenge to seek and encourage the public to become contributors for this book.

It was a welcome challenge to 'help' those with commitment issues that needed a little extra encouragement to actually get started and a little more of the same to get the person to complete their story.

The flipside was that the potential contributors were encouraging *me* to *hassle* them to get their experiences written down. Their reasons were many and varied, to keep putting this task off, of which some are listed below:

- Trying to get off their medication altogether, changing medication or reducing dosages
- Trying too hard and fizzling out
- Bouncing back and forth from controlling their addictions
- Feelings being overloaded from remembering and expressing their experiences. Many contributors spent years to decades trying to forget their 'past' and/or current situation.
- Real intention to write their story for the book, as they have had previous desire to do so and had not yet succeeded. The extra initiative was a motivational key.

Although not all 'contributor enquires' ended up being successful in submitting their experiences, the courage and interest to spark a contact was a big step for the person, nonetheless. The interest in general, generated a renewed thought process to 'stop-feel-think' about what they are going through and why. At this point, many people could not pass on their experiences and decided not to pursue the project any further. For these people, writing a story highlighting experiences of their mental health problem/s turned it all into a 'too real' situation giving an overall sensation of overwhelming unbearableness and exposed their raw feelings of not being able to cope writing their story.

The portrayal of the 'endlessness' in this situation was enough to frighten the individuals into surrendering, and leaving them feeling powerless. Hence, these people were obviously not ready to face this challenge in this manner, and as a consequence, gave the power back to their mental health problem.

On the other hand, for many people, the timing to write down their experiences was only a little short of perfect. This made my idea for the book a reality that people were interested and wanted to share their experiences to help others be aware of their mental condition and consequences.

Now, I had the extra 'pressure' to be successful in getting the book published because it would mean so much to the contributors to know that their real stories were being read and remembered.

When the stories did come in, I was genuinely and pleasantly surprised by the 'realness' of the experiences. Not one of the contributors tried to create an illusion of turning their mental health problems into a joke or a passing, unimportant phase or that the individual was unaffected by the consequences of diagnosis and so on.

This 'mature' and realistic approach impressed me and featured across the diverse age groups amongst the contributors. But, as the reader will discover, the contributors are real people with real daily challenges that not always reflected the committed approach that they required to undertake this project.

Mental health problems for not only the contributors, but for the community as a whole, continues to be challenged, long and beyond the time this book was completed. The support needed in these situations does not stop here; it must be ongoing, appropriate, respectful, reliable and resilient.

Mental Health Problems Overview – Quick Reference

This is a simplified version of descriptions of mental health problems. It is not designed to be used as an assessment or diagnostic tool, but rather a reference to help the reader gain some insight of the mental health concerns contained within the contributor's stories, and/or clarify some misconceptions and confusion between some mental health issues/illness/disorders.

I hope not to offend anyone because I have simplified this overview of mental health problems or that I have only included some of them in this book. For a detailed and in depth meanings, descriptions, manifestations, therapy and treatments, please refer to well-reputed references whether person, book or online sources. A good place to start in regards to personality disorders is the DSM-IV (Diagnostic and Statistical Manual of Mental Disorders), a psychiatric reference manual. It is a diagnostic tool used worldwide and classes disorders into clusters of 'odd/eccentric', 'dramatic/emotional/erratic', 'anxious/fearful' or 'unspecified'.

Take note that the symptoms listed here in this book are mainly those exhibited by adults, unless otherwise specified; as symptoms often differ between those of children and adults.

The reader may be tempted to self-diagnose, 'that sounds like me,' scenario. Under no circumstances is that acceptable, seek professional advice for assessment, diagnosis, therapy and treatment. In saying that, it is a positive outcome if the reader can identify and relate to certain parts of this book. Self –awareness is the key to gaining a real perspective on mental health problems and what that means, for the future, to the individual seeking advice and strategies.

Simply Defined

- 'Professionals' – refers to those who work in the mental health field, whether in the clinic, school environment, academia, organisation profit and/or non-for-profit, hospital, and research department. To name a few are; counsellors, psychologists, psychiatrists, social workers, psychiatric nurses, psychotherapists, theorists and behaviour analysts.

- 'Mental Health' – is a term used to express the psychological wellbeing of an individual, how they generally cope on a daily basis, performing everyday tasks.

- 'Mental health problems' – is a collective term covering the scope of mental health issues, illness and disorders. It refers to a psychological deviation from the stable and well-adjusted individual in everyday situations and/or 'under pressure.' These deviations can be displayed in the form of behaviour, speech, thought patterns, non-verbal cues and so on.

- 'Mental health issues' – tends to refer to the 'short term' life problems experienced by people. An example is when someone close to you dies, the living family members, relatives, friends and work colleagues may suffer from depression. A time passing in the wake of loneliness and change in daily routine, until gradually the healing process helps with the loss of the loved one. Mental health issues vary accordingly from person to person, not just in description but intensity. Depending on the disposition of the individual, certain mental health issues can trigger underlying, unresolved, unidentified and/or undiagnosed mental health illnesses/disorders.

- 'Mental illness and mental disorder' – are commonly interchangeable terms. There are some professionals that suggest 'mental disorder' should be used when the origin is biologically/neurologically based and 'mental illnesses' should be used when mental problem is environmentally based. This is in itself a debate, 'nature versus nurture,' has been in contention for decades now. With a deeper understanding and knowledge surrounding these issues, through medical research and the like, many new discoveries have been found or previous discoveries corrected. It has been strongly suggested with scientific proof for backup, that schizophrenia disorder is a biologically based mental health problem. This leads to the conclusion that the person is born with it, a 'nature' contender. It is around the forty years of age, that the average individual is diagnosed with schizophrenia, although there are those diagnosed with a form of schizophrenia at around the age of twenty. Having this knowledge allows the professional to treat accordingly, to treat the chemical imbalance in the individual's brain with medication. Therapy helps the individual also in other ways, but combining the two, therapy and treatment, the person diagnosed with schizophrenia disorder can live a happy and fulfilling life.

Not to confuse this too much, but syndrome and disorder are often interchangeable terms, mainly this is subjective to geographical location, i.e. Australia, America, United Kingdom, Europe etc. Over the years, with more funding for research and a better working knowledge of mental health problems, a lot of professionals (and the general public) have changed their viewpoint from 'all in the mind' to 'disorder.' Hence Post Traumatic Stress, Depression, Addiction and Anxiety problems were all classed as 'all in the mind.' Now, it's Post Traumatic Stress Disorder, Depressive Disorders, Eating Disorders, Bipolar Disorder just to name a few.

All this change to date has brought about serious funding and interest nearly the world over; to help people diagnosed with mental health problems to seek affordable assistance in and out of the hospital setting, with less judgement and ridicule from the general community. Although in recent times, there has been more social awareness governing how to be supportive rather than stigmatise, those individuals that need help with their mental health problem, to do so freely and with as much dignity as possible, ignorance in the community still exists. Nearly all of the contributor's stories exhibit how cruel society around them can be, to those with mental health problems, instead of showing respect, empathy, patience and understanding.

Post-Traumatic Stress Disorder is diagnosed when a person has experienced such a traumatic event in their lives, that they repeatedly relive the experience. This re-experience can be during day or night. Fear and anxiety becomes a constant factor in their lives and panic soon takes over. Returned soldiers, abuse victims, fire fighters, ambulance officers and police officers are just a few categories of those most likely to expose themselves to horrific situations and suffer PTSD.

POST-TRAUMATIC STRESS DISORDER (PTSD)

Common Symptoms

- Panic attacks
- Flashbacks
- Irritability
- Anger
- Confusion
- Suicidal tendencies
- Powerlessness which sometimes is confused with laziness or inadequacy as a partner/father/breadwinner
- May turn to substance abuse to regain control or to 'block/black out' memories

PTSD is usually associated with poor or non-responsiveness to most therapy treatments available. Constant support and patience is very much required by those who are in immediate environment of a sufferer.

SOCIAL ANXIETY DISORDER

Common Symptoms

- Exhibits an expression of embarrassment
- Fidgeting
- Racing heart
- Ability to talk is compromised due to dry mouth and extreme nervousness
- As children typically known as 'shy', which carries through to adulthood

People with this disorder have strong sensitivities toward most or all social interactions. It is a very traumatic experience for them, every time, with feelings of being terrified, anxious and fear of rejection. Low self-esteem is prevalent and a good starting point for therapy.

Social Anxiety Disorder is also known as 'Social Phobia.' Phobias in general are classed as anxiety disorders, for obvious reasons, the level of anxiety are dramatic and sustained until trigger is removed. Some other kinds of phobias are fear of spiders, confined spaces, red coloured foods, driving/being in a vehicle, thunderstorms, public speaking and needles (injections.)

People diagnosed with this disorder exhibit a variety of thoughts and behaviours in conjunction with a stand-out symptom of performing repetitive tasks to the point that it becomes a daily ritual. This form of thinking and behaviour patterns are programmed by fear. The fear of germs 'makes' the individual perform repetitive tasks of cleaning, hand washing and/or wearing protective gear like face masks and disposable gloves. The fear of not doing things right is another example of OCD, which 'drives' the person to constantly move items around and/or making sure there is order and arranging the items the same way. Any deviation from any of this highly interferes with their anxiety levels and increases the likelihood of performing the tasks even more often.

OBSESSIVE-COMPULSIVE DISORDER (OCD)

Common Symptoms

- Repetitive tasks, daily
- Ritualistic patterns
- The urge to always be collecting or hoarding
- Obsessive

OCD sufferers have 'obsessions' which is whatever they fear, like germs. The repetitive tasks they then perform are called 'compulsions' which is the washing of hands and so on. This individual is convinced that the more the hand washing is performed, the less likely there will be germs. Hence, a vicious cycle is exercised by their fear and perpetuated by their anxiety to be rid of the germs.

GENERALISED ANXIETY DISORDER (GAD)

Common Symptoms

- Over anxiety
- Excessive worry without provocation
- Inability to relax and be still

People diagnosed with GAD display excessive amounts of worry and nervousness over trivial, unprovoked occurrences and what may potentially happen in certain situations. Their thought patterns extend to "This could happen…" scenario and develop unrealistic reasoning to substantiate their reactive behaviour.

People with Generalised Anxiety Disorder are very difficult to be around and support, as they constantly express their extreme and unreasonable anxieties about things, no matter the consequence.

Anxiety and Panic Disorders have a lot of common general symptoms like fear, anxiety, nervousness and panic. Over time and more research, Mental Health professionals have been able to better distinguish between these disorders and structure therapy and treatment accordingly. One of these facts is that these kinds of disorders preludes or precedes other types, like Eating or Depressive Disorders.

CLINICAL DEPRESSION

Common Symptoms

- Unfocussed at home, work and socially
- Avoids leaving the house at all costs
- Unexplained tiredness
- Strong feelings of failure
- Unmotivated
- May be found still in bed in the afternoon
- Feelings of sadness more often than not
- Unwilling to seek enjoyment, whether old or new
- Suicidal tendencies, attempts and/or speech
- Substance abuse, may have been 'using' prior

Sometimes referred to as Major Depressive Disorder, people diagnosed with this have experienced depressive symptoms for a long time with an elevated intensity. On a daily basis, the individual may experience for example, severe feelings of sadness and low self-esteem or unmotivated to the extent that not even getting their children ready for school or themselves for work is going to get them out of bed. Recurrent suicidal tendencies are also common, usually having the opposite support and care factor from those that are around them often. It gets to a stage where friends, work colleagues, school friends and family members stop believing them and in them, and accepts the fact that the person is not suffering a real mental illness but just seeking unnecessary attention. That is when the individual in question usually succeeds in ending their life; they feel at their lowest and the most alone. On the other hand, there have been lots of situations in which a new friend or acquaintance will 'see' the 'cry for help' and offer helpful advice and support. Many depressed people have been assisted out of depression by new partners, new friends, relatives that they have not seen for a while and acquaintances.

Clinical Depression whether mild, moderate or severe, can be diagnosed as early as two weeks. Immediate professional help and support from family and friends will encourage recovery sooner without the chance of manifestations, i.e. substance abuse, self-harm and so on. This disorder can be broken down into further categories depending on additional symptoms. For Example:

PSYCHOTIC DEPRESSION:

The person diagnosed with this type of depression experiences delusions or hallucinations and has lost the ability to 'see' reason and reality. Severe mood swings are common with low times (depression) and high times (mania).

MELANCHOLIA DEPRESSION:

With Melancholia Depression a person experiences dramatic amounts of sadness and low self-esteem. The fear of failure is the most common symptom which leads to the feelings of inadequateness and melancholia. Hence mood swings are practically non-existent as the person is mostly and daily feeling sad, i.e. low times dominate.

There are numerous other types and reasons for depression. Some has very specific symptoms due to situational influences, as listed below:

- New family member, newborn baby
- Partner, family or close friend as recently passed away
- Bankruptcy
- Moved away from friends and school
- Separation and/or divorce
- Medical diagnosis that is overwhelming, i.e. cancer, needing organ transplant etc.
- Seasonal changes, i.e. lack of sunlight

In recent times, extensive study and research has produced convincing results that a person maybe more prone to suffering some type of depression in their lifetime over another individual due to a heredity influence. Hence, there is a strong family indication, such as mother and daughter with depression.

ANOREXIA NERVOSA DISORDER

Common Symptoms

- Eating and drinking only a little
- Days of not eating and/or drinking
- Losing a lot weight
- Excessive body hair
- Regular 'mirror' watching
- Very little energy, stamina, Strength and recovery
- Excessive exercise
- Skeletal skinniness

Anorexia Nervosa affects both males and females across all ages. It is characterised by the unhealthy and unrealistic outlook with self-image issues and/or food issues. This causes the person to lose weight and keep losing weight. Keeping the weight off eventually becomes an obsession as it is associated with the person's 'comfort' zone.

For some sufferers Anorexia Nervosa is a lifelong battle, with episodes of 'on' and 'off' throughout their lives. Although there are those who recover fully within a few years, there are those who lose the battle and die. While the individual that recovered from the disorder no longer starves themselves skinny, they may have caused long term damage to their heart, muscles, stomach and so on. It is a devastating disorder, without doubt, which also has repercussions that reach those that love and care for them, especially family members.

BULIMA DISORDER

People who are Bulimic ritualistically have sessions of eating and not eating. When they do eat, it is in the form of uncontrollable binging. After binging most will force the food back up in order to stay thin and not gain weight. Some people use laxatives instead of vomiting. Some use both methods.

Common Symptoms

- Days of not eating at all
- Days of nibbling at food
- Episodes of binging
- Chewing gum often to mask bad breath from vomiting
- Regular 'mirror' watching
- May manifest into substance abuse
- Alternate weight loss, then weight gain
- Unrealistic body image issues

It is an 'in the closet' Eating Disorder, as many family members and close friends are oblivious that the individual performs these rituals in order to remain thin. Usually Bulimics are caught in the act of binging, such as sitting in front of the fridge with the door wide open, eating without pause. Or they get found out because after a meal a family member or friend has picked up on the routine of them going to the bathroom straight after eating, to vomit. Hence when the person is confronted, an admission is usually made, that they are in the habit of getting rid of what they eat, after the fact, in order to stay thin. Like Anorexia Nervosa, this disorder can be a lifelong battle with episodic periods, and some Bulimics may recover fully after just months or years.

Many people who have experienced an Eating Disorder realise years later whether the initial cause/trigger was 'social' based or 'anxiety' based. An exact timeline can then be plotted which in turn, provides a revelation of greater understanding of 'why?' rather than 'why me?'

PANIC DISORDER

Common Symptoms
(During a panic attack)

- Dizzy
- Unable to take a deep breath
- Temporary paralysis
- Confusion
- Loss of control
- Blurry vision
- Heart racing

A person diagnosed with Panic Disorder experiences fear and anxiety in the form of panic attacks. It is self-perpetuating, as the person fears and gets even more anxious of repeat attacks. This is because the very first attack was an unpleasant surprise and the cause/trigger unknown. For those who suffer panic attacks, some of the common thoughts are that they will die, never be able to take a deep breath and/or faint. For people diagnosed with this disorder, each and every panic attack is extremely overwhelming, leaving them panic stricken with fear. Some people only experience the one attack, others experience them for years.

Some people have their first panic attack in a public place and quickly establish an association between the two. This is called Panic Disorder with Agoraphobia. The result here is they do not leave home at all, or they try not being very far from home. They also avoid that particular public place because of the strong feelings of anxiety and fear of experiencing another panic attack. Common public areas seem to be the beach, large shopping complexes, the library, working behind the counter serving customers, exam time, restaurants/cafes, the dentist/doctor surgery and nightclubs or just being outdoors in the backyard.

PASSIVE AGGRESSIVE DISORDER

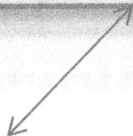

Passive Aggressive is a disorder that affects people's view of things and subsequent behaviour. The sufferer exhibits negative attitudes but with a passive approach to resistance. Their views are very much an obstruction in interpersonal situations with no follow-through or compromise.

Common Symptoms

- Hostile 'nature'
- A lot of dialogue that is reflective of negative attitudes
- No resistance, takes the 'back seat'
- Comes across as being uncaring, useless, forgetful and very lazy.

The partners, family and friends of those with Passive Aggressive Disorder, find it very frustrating to live with or 'deal' with someone that constantly has a negative attitude and displays hostility. Every activity becomes an unpleasant chore between them and in turn perpetuates the hostility that surrounds the Passive Aggressive individual. This is a very challenging environment that requires professional intervention of therapy and treatment, for the individual in question and those close to them, on a daily basis, such as family members.

OPPOSITIONAL DEFIANT DISORDER (ODD)

Common Symptoms

- Shows hostility and disrespect towards any authority figure
- Prefers to be alone
- Has difficulty interacting with people, whether family or those within the school environment
- Has difficulty following instructions
- ODD is diagnosed from as early as childhood.

It is characterised by behaviours showing hostility and disregard towards authority figures. Hence many times teachers and/or support staff at school pick up on it in the first instance. Many parents and/or carers are informed by the school that their child is displaying certain antisocial behaviours. From there, identification and treatment can follow, instructed by a suitable qualified professional and supervised at home and school. It is a personality disorder which left untreated, will usually progress into a violent form called Conduct Disorder.

CONDUCT DISORDER (CD)

Common Symptoms

- Lying
- Cheating
- Stealing
- Violence
- General criminal activity
- Strong disregard for the law and authority figures
- Delinquency
- Signs of irresponsibility
- Substance abuse

ODD children are usually diagnosed with CD at the older age childhood spectrum. This is when ODD behaviours become consistently more violent, aggressive and 'uncontrollable.' Left untreated the child will develop antisocial behaviours, that after the age of eighteen years, Antisocial Personality Disorder (ASPD) will be diagnosed. Treatment and/or rehabilitation become less successful as the stages of CD to ASPD establish the person's 'comfort' zone. This comfort zone, whether socially acceptable or not, becomes the main focus and not much can interfere here without negative consequence.

BORDERLINE PERSONALITY DISORDER

A person diagnosed with this disorder exhibits a very rigid thought pattern structure that allows no flexibility. This type of 'thinking' affects the person and their surroundings, whether at work, at home or leisure activities. A lot of anxiety and powerlessness is self-generated here and usually the person tries to gain or regain control by substance abuse, self-harm activities or binge-eating to name a few.

Common Symptoms

- Non-flexible way of thinking – i.e. no compromising etc.
- Can be self-harmers
- Show anxiety symptoms when things do not go to plan despite effort involved
- Unstable emotions
- Fluctuation regarding actions and reactions – i.e. 'I hate you. Don't leave me.'

HISTRIONIC PERSONALITY DISORDER

People diagnosed with Histrionic Personality Disorder are constantly seeking attention, no matter the situation or the environment. They prefer to physically 'seduce' to gain the attention they desire and think they deserve. They constantly exercise inappropriate behaviour in order to achieve their goal of being the centre of attention. Hence, this is their 'comfort zone', so at all costs; the individual will 'do' what is necessary to achieve this.

Common Symptoms

- Shallowness
- 'Seducer' label
- Emotionally dramatic
- 'Drama Queen' label

It is known, from many years of studying people with 'Personality Disorders' that the intensity of symptoms reduces markedly with age. This is good news not only for the individual with the disorder but their family and friends.

In Narcissistic Personality Disorder, the person displays an overinflated opinion of themselves, creating a 'fantasy surround.' This assists them to feel important, and do not want to be reminded that they are one of millions of human beings on the planet. Being humble is not one of their strengths. They emotionally feed on others to satisfy their strong desire for admiration and recognition. It is a big task to fill for those people around them to continuously 'bow down' and pamper the narcissist's every nuance. Hence, individuals with this disorder are quite often very difficult company and commonly have only a small group of friends, if any.

NARCISSISTIC PERSONALITY DISORDER

Common Symptoms

- Lack of empathy
- Fluctuating emotions
- Strong signals of jealousy
- 'In your face,' personality
- Unrealistic self-importance

BIPOLAR DISORDER I AND II

Someone with Bipolar has a general and constant uneasiness of how they feel about themselves. There are mood swings from feeling 'high' to feeling 'low'. Each high and low varies in length from hours to days and the intensity from mild, moderate or severe. With Bipolar Disorder I these mood swings are very high and very low, lasting longer in duration than individuals diagnosed with Bipolar Disorder II. In Bipolar II, the mania (high) is absent or if present is not of such a high intensity; in this form it is called Hypomania. Also, the in-between times the individual can lead a relatively normal life, uninterrupted or governed by their condition, compared with people diagnosed with Bipolar Disorder I.

Common Symptoms

- Mania (high), BP I
- Depression (low), BP I and II
- Mood swings, BP I – extreme, BP II – mild
- A seemingly lack of need to sleep, eat and relax
- Erratic speech, BP I
- Happy episodes
- Anger episodes
- Bouts of energy
- Bouts of sadness
- Bouts of tiredness
- Crying
- Low self-esteem
- Low social awareness i.e. becomes less social or stops 'going out' altogether
- During mania and depressive episodes, may experience hallucinations (seeing, hearing, feeling) and/or be delusional (unfounded or false beliefs), BP I

People with Bipolar are said to be very creative and artistic well above the norm, some of which are classed as geniuses in this field.

SCHIZOPHRENIA

Common Symptoms

- Odd physical movements
- Odd speech style – fast, slow, slurry to indecipherable
- Basic body hygiene is very poor
- Odd behaviour
- Odd and false thoughts and feelings
- Lack of fluidity in speech, thought and 'mental storage' of what is seen and heard.
- Delusional
- Visual and auditory hallucinations

There are many types of Schizophrenia depending on the range of symptoms, behaviours and feelings that the individual exhibits. For example, if a deep sense and subsequent behaviour of paranoia is strongly indicated, this is typically referred to as Paranoid Schizophrenia. Disorganised Schizophrenia is diagnosed when a young person presents with typical symptoms of Schizophrenia, at around the age of twenty, rather than the common diagnosis age of forty. People with this disorder typically experience psychosis. This means that delusions and/or hallucinations are prevalent throughout their lifetime.

Schizophrenics can reduce the severity of their symptoms with treatment, especially in the form of medication. Over the years, this has helped numerous sufferers to be able to 'live around or with' their disorder and pursue their goals of family, leisure, social and/or work orientations.

Currently, Schizophrenia is labelled a psychotic disorder whereas Bipolar is commonly referred to as a mood disorder. The differences between the two are quite vast and only a few symptoms are similar. Many people have been misdiagnosed because, in the past, these two disorders were thought to be 'one and the same'.

Here is a basic outline of the differences between the two disorders which will help to give an insight of the uniqueness of each and hopefully lessen the confusion.

- Bipolar Disorder affects how a person views themselves
- Schizophrenia affects how a person views others

- Most of the time, people with Bipolar express happiness, joy, anger, and sadness through laughing, smiling, raised voices and crying during spells between their lows and highs, at appropriate cues.
- People with Schizophrenia may express these same emotions and behaviours but at inappropriate times. For example, laughing hysterically at a funeral. With some individuals, they have an inability to express themselves at all. This makes it a challenge for those who surround them on a daily basis, whether family, friends or work colleagues.

- Bipolar sufferers have 'normal' spells between highs and lows which can last any length of time. This gives them the freedom to function adequately on a day to day basis.
- Schizophrenics have major issues with interpreting the world around them, what is real and what is not, visually and on an auditory level. Making the fluidity of thought and speech a challenge for those around them. Hence, communication is problematic.

- Bipolar Disorder tends to have heightened or lowered variations of 'normal' movements, behaviour, speech and thought during mood swings.
- People diagnosed with Schizophrenia tend to have odd ways of thinking, moving, behaving and talking.

Pornography   **INTERNET**   Hard
Drugs   Pharmaceutical Drugs
SHOPLIFTING   Hoarding
Soft drugs   Coke a Cola
Cigarettes   Stealing   **Alcohol**
Food   Social Media
Specific Colours, like pink is a common
one.   **PETROCHEMICALS**
Sunbathing – natural or solariums
Consuming 'non-foods' i.e. laundry
powder, chalk, glass, toilet paper
etc.

ADDICTION

People can be addicted to just about anything. There are common addictions which are mainly due to the addictive qualities of the substance, action, feel, taste and/or 'look' that the human body can be particularly susceptible to.

The 'high' the individual experiences whether it's from cocaine or chocolate, keeps them wanting…needing…craving more. The intensity of the craving and the frequency of the action become more urgent and increases in incidence. Both the craving and the action play a major role in any addiction. It is quiet common that the addicts that have stopped drinking alcohol, for example, whether for weeks or decades, will also miss the action of physically drinking and being in an atmosphere to drink. It was a 'world' they created and felt comfortable or safe in, untouchable from the misery they faced when feeling sober. Hence, it made reality less demanding, despite the fact that their 'modified' reality was hindering any chance to redeem what was lost, whether family, money, job, health and/or power/control.

It is very challenging for any addict to firstly admit that they are an addict and secondly, to actively seek professional help to counteract both the craving and the action of addiction.

According to many addicts, once reformed, admit that it is true, 'once an addict always an addict.' For example, a cocaine addict that has reformed will on a daily basis think about cocaine, but not use. It is a daily ordeal that society in general, would not wish upon another person. Addiction is very consuming and can be devastating for the people close to the addict.

ANTISOCIAL PERSONALITY DISORDER (ASPD)

ASPD is characterised by a complete disregard for socially acceptable behaviours and norms. These people are risk takers for fun and have no real concept of how their actions may affect the people around them and/or their victims. Frustration can quickly turn into aggression and horrific violent acts can be a result. Regular criminal activity is common. Because of the complexity of ASPD and consequential lack of empathy, treatment is rarely successful. People with this disorder do not understand why they need treatment, as far as they are concerned, everything is fine and rehabilitation is irrelevant. Therefore, because of this, they rarely seek treatment and if they do, rarely commit. Adults with ASPD usually have been diagnosed with Conduct Disorder (CD) from childhood. CD left undiagnosed and/or untreated will result in the child progressing to ASPD.

Common Symptoms
- Lack of empathy
- Disrespect for the rights of others
- Regular criminal activity
- Non-committal i.e. moves address a lot, name changes, quits jobs regularly
- Unable to form meaningful, long-term relationships
- Prefers to be alone
- Short, clipped way of speaking
- Liar
- Easily frustrated, which usually leads to violence

People diagnosed with ASPD are mistakenly referred to as psychopaths or sociopaths. Psychopathy for example, exhibits symptoms that include those of ASPD but **also** traits that represent manipulation, egocentricity, shallowness and a genuine lack of guilt and remorse. Notice the word 'traits' is used here, this is because these symptoms are not environmentally influenced but 'hard-wired' from birth, as the popular, professional opinion stands today. Hence, ASPD is only a part of psychopathy, but not in the whole sense, as those with ASPD are not necessarily psychopaths.

Keeping Mental Health -Healthy

Some people, professionals or otherwise, might say that this is a very idealistic viewpoint full of assumptions and based on inaccurate understanding of 'human nature'. To some extent this is correct. Not everyone wants to commit to keeping their mental health in check. This requires support, understanding, accepting help whether professional or not, vigilance, dedication, determination, acceptance, inspiration, motivation and honesty to name a few.

Keeping mental health, healthy is a daily challenge but with the right 'tools' and mindset it is achievable. From my personal and professional experience, this 'task' becomes less like a chore, easier with time and practise; and the rewards far outweigh the effort involved.

By no means is the individual's creativity, uniqueness or personality put in jeopardy. This is not about standardising mental health for each and every one, more like stabilising it and focussing understanding. After all it is achieving a deeper understanding of what 'makes' the person an individual, strengths, weaknesses and all. This takes the guesswork out of most situations, whether it is deciding which job better suits their skills and personality to choosing the most suitable partner for long term relationships.

The right 'tools' are subjective. They are dependent on many aspects, some of which are the age of the individual, the mental capacity of understanding what is 'socially acceptable' for right and wrong in that particular geographical location, culture, situation and external pressures.

Here is an example

A young person has their VCE exams coming up and typically becomes extremely anxious prior, during and after any exam period. There is vomiting, muscle aches, headaches, reduced appetite, sleeplessness, decreased concentration, tiredness, moodiness and social withdrawal. If the young person accepts that all of this is just part of their response to the stress of exams and feels the extra pressure to perform, there is a good chance this response will be better managed and in turn produce favourable results.   Hence, acceptance and understanding here allows an opportunity to modulate and produce better exam results and less reactive symptoms from the anxiety.

In this particular example, the right 'tools' for this person can be as follows:

- Making a study plan tailored to specific needs and after school activities
- Plan to start studying weeks before the exams, allowing no chance for last minute cramming, inviting confusion and unnecessary panic
- Try not to over study; it is just as 'bad' as understudying. It typically allows a higher incidence of silly mistakes to be made which is very costly in the overall marking of exam papers
- Allow for study 'blocks' on weekends, to be shared with a study partner or study group for particularly difficult or high-loaded information subjects
- Ask parents for permission to get professional assistance from a qualified tutor if needed
- Make time to break up the study with things like walking the dog, family outings, go out with friends, go for a run, swim, cook, listen to music etc.
- Try to eat and sleep according to the 'usual' routine

Deciphering and practising what works for the individual with the help of a supportive team of family and friends, seeking professional assistance if necessary and setting realistic goals, is a healthy start towards maintaining mental health.

Conclusion

Whatever mental health problems are in question, the person suffering or surviving the issue or disorder should be the main focus. Their individuality, their strengths and weaknesses should help with determining the right and most effective 'tools' for therapy and treatment. As displayed in this book by the contributor's real stories of their experiences, their livelihood, personality and creativity depends on it. The rest of the community should engage in encouraging support and non-judgemental assistance, without prejudice and misunderstanding. You never know, it could affect you one day, your partner, your child, your best friend…

There are those who have turned their lives around to live a fulfilling existence, encompassing their mental health problems with respect and using what they can, on a daily basis, to be constructive and positive.

And there are those that have the lost that 'battle'.

'Be thine own Palace, or the world's thy jail'
John Donne (1572-1631)

References

http://health.discovery.com/tv/psych-week
"Discovery Fit & Health – it's about life…your life," 2012

http://bluepages.anu.edu.au/symptoms/experiences
"Famous People" The Centre for Mental Health Research, the Australian National University, 2001/2006

http://en.wikipedia.org/wiki
"List of people with bipolar disorder," last modified 13th January 2013

http://www.healthyplace.com/thought-disorder/schizophrenia
"Famous People with Schizophrenia – Confirmed Cases," Reviewed by Harry Croft, MD, Psychologist, 2012

"The Complete Autobiography" Janet Frame (1924-2004), Pub date 1990 by Women's Press

http://en.wikipedia.org/wiki
"Mental health Professional," 2010

http://www.healthinsite.gov.au/topics
"Anxiety Disorder," CRUfAD, Healthinsite, October 2011

http://www.anxietynetwork.com/content
"Anxiety Disorder Definitions," The Anxiety Network, by Thomas A. Richards, Psychologist

http://www.webmd.com/anxiety-panic/guide
"Obsessive-Compulsive Disorder," WebMD, Reviewed by Marina Katz, MD, 20th February 2012

http://www.betterhealth.vic.gov.au
"Depression – different types," Better Health Channel in consultation with and approved by beyondblue, last reviewed 1st February 2013

http://au.reachout.com
"Bipolar Disorder," REACHOUT.com

Agata Zema

http://www.nlm.nih.gov/medlineplus
"Psychotic Disorders," 16th October 2012, "Schizophrenia," 23rd February 2013, MedlinePlus - Trusted Health Information for You, US National Library of Medicine, US Department of Health and Human Services, National Institutes of Health

http://psychcentral.com
"Borderline Personality Disorder," 2007, "Histrionic Personality Disorder," 9th July 2012, PsychCentral – Learn.Share.Grow, Psych Central Staff and reviewed by John M. Grohol Psy.D.

http://www.mentalhealthaustralia.net
"Antisocial personality disorder," Mental Health Australia, 2007

http://www.goodreads.com/quotes
"John Donne > Quotes," Goodreads Inc., 2013

Acknowledgements

A big and warm thank you to all the contributors, your unique stories are invaluable.

Without you, this book never would have come to fruition or be anywhere near as good.

Thanks to the wonderful photography performed by Amber, PMPM Photography (Precious Moments, Priceless Memories Photography),your talent is outstanding. Thank you for sharing.

Big thanks to Don K for giving up a lot of time and sleep to organise manuscript layout in RTF.

My mum, dad and sisters; thank you for your support and unending love.

Our son; for letting me take breaks from the book for feeding and give-me-attention time.

My partner; for all his love, care and support without one word or action to the contrary. Thank you for your patience.

www.ingramcontent.com/pod-product-compliance
Lightning Source LLC
Chambersburg PA
CBHW031219270326
41931CB00006B/618